W9-BJS-378

# Questions
## *about Slovenia*

Everything you wanted to know about Slovenia...
... and you had nowhere to ask.

Založba Turistika
Kranj, 2003

QUESTIONS ABOUT SLOVENIA
Everything you wanted to know about Slovenia...
... and you had nowhere to ask.

Researched, compiled, adapted and written by: Matjaž Chvatal
Translator: Vanja Živkovič Fric
Lecturer: Stephen Corston
Photos by: Matjaž Chvatal, Arne Hodalič, Bogdan Kladnik, Egon
Kaše, Martina Pogornik, Rolf Lindeman, Borut Lozej …

Publisher:
Turistika Publising House, 2003
For the publisher: Mira Chvatal

Založba Turistika
Trstenik 101
4204 Golnik
e-mail: info@zalozba-turistika.si
http://www.zalozba-turistika.si

CIP – Kataložni zapis o publikaciji
Narodna in univerzitetna knjižnica, Ljubljana

908(497.4)

CHVATAL, Matjaž
  Questions about Slovenia : everything you wanted to know about
Slovenia --- and you had nowhere to ask / (reserched, compiled,
adapted and written by Matjaž Chvatal ; photos by Matjaž Chvatal ...
et al.) ; translator Vanja Živkovič Fric). - Golnik : Turistika, 2003

Izv. nasl.: Vprašanja o Sloveniji

ISBN 961-6414-03-8

# Questions
## *about Slovenia*

Everything you wanted to know about Slovenia...
... and you had nowhere to ask.

# Facts and Figures

# How densely populated are Slovene towns?

**Capital**: Ljubljana (270,000 inhabitants);
**Other big towns**: Maribor (114,000), Kranj (51,800), Celje (48,400), Koper (48,000), Novo mesto (41,000), Nova Gorica (36,000), Velenje (34,000), Kamnik (26,000), Ptuj (24,000), Škofja Loka (22,000), Jesenice (22,000), Murska Sobota (20,000);

Ljubljana

Maribor

Kranj

Celje

Koper

# What is the difference between Slovenia, Slovakia and Slavonia?

People often get these three countries mixed up due to their similar names and their position in Central Europe. However, Slovenia and Slovakia are independent countries and Slavonia is a region in the northeast of Croatia.
Those not used to Slavic languages can easily confuse them as the Slovene, Croatian (spoken in Slavonia) and Slovak languages are, though very similar in sound, quite different in meaning.

# Where is Slovenia and what is it like?

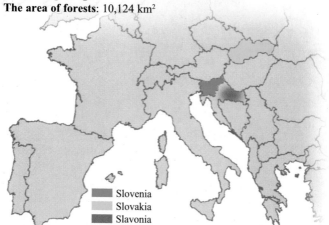

**Location**: Slovenia is a Central European state.

**Area**: 20,273 km²

**The length of its borders**: with Austria 330km, Italy 232km, Hungary 102km and Croatia 670 km; a total of 1,334 km.

**Coastline**: 46.6 km

**The highest mountain**: Triglav – 2,864 m

**Waters**: Slovenia is rich in waters. The total length of its watercourses, rivers, constant and torrent feeder streams is 26,600 km. Its total amount of fluvial water per capita makes Slovenia one of the richest European countries as it exceeds the European average by almost four times.

**The average height above the sea level**: 556.8 m

**The area of forests**: 10,124 km²

- Slovenia
- Slovakia
- Slavonia

# Where are Slovenia's natural and landscape parks?

1. Boč
2. the valley of the Dragonja
3. Čaven–the plateau Trnovski gozd
4. The Glinščica
5. The Golte
6. Goričko
7. The Snežnik Castle
8. The Jeruzalem hilly district
9. The Karavanke mountain range and The Kamnik Alps
10. The Kolpa
11. The Kozjansko region
12. The Kras
13. The Lahinja
14. Lipica
15. The Ljubljana Marshes
16. The valley of Logarska dolina
17. The Martuljek chain
18. The Mašun
19. The Mura dead arms
20. Nanos
21. lake Negovsko jezero
22. The Planinsko polje valley
23. Porezen
24. The Rakov Škocjan
25. The Robanov kot valley
26. The Sečovlje saltpans
27. Strunjan
28. The Škocjan Caves
29. Štanjel
30. Štatenberg
31. Tivoli park-Rožnik-Šišenski hrib
32. Triglav National Park
33. The Topla
34. Vremščica
35. The Upper Idrijca

Nanos

Jeruzalem hill district

Strunjan

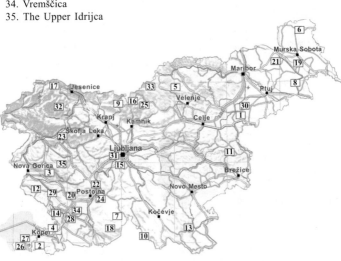

# What are the protected areas?

About 8% of the total area is protected.

**The Triglav National Park** covers the largest area (83,807 ha) in the central region of the Slovene Julian Alps and ranges from the rugged highlands to the cultivated areas. Tourist centres are: Bovec, Kranjska Gora, Bled, Bohinj.

A NATIONAL PARK is a great area abundant in numerous natural gems and diverse biotic potential. The larger part of the national park reveals unexploited nature with its preserved ecosystems and natural processes. The smaller part can be more greatly influenced by man but still harmonious with nature.

A REGIONAL PARK is a large area of ecosystems characteristic of both a region and countryside with large sections of unspoilt nature and areas of natural beauty intermingled with parts more greatly affected by man and still in balance with nature.

A LANDSCAPE PARK is an area where a quality and long-term co-existence between man and nature is particularly visible and is of great ecologic, biotic and scenic value.

**The Škocjan Caves** are a typical example of contact karst caves. The river Reka, Slovenia's longest disappearing river, first eroded a 2 km long surface canyon and then an underground one in the Škocjan Caves. This underground river resurfaces in the near-by cave Kačna jama, the abyss Labodnica in Italy and as the river Timav in the Gulf of Trieste.

**The Sečovelje saltpanes** are one of the northernmost saltpanes in the Mediterranean basin. Their partly preserved traditional way of salt making is unique to this area. There are as many as 45 Slovene endangered floral species growing here. Additionally, for birds the saltpanes are an important nesting ground (80 species), intermediate migrating stop and wintering area (more than 200 species have been sighted here).

# What are the connections between the domestic and foreign markets?

The Slovene economy is open to business with foreign markets. Slovenia is a member state of the WTO.
Approximately 2/3 of its trade is conducted with the European Union.

**Slovenian exports:**
Driving machines and farm machinery
Metal processing devices
Electrical engines
Vehicles
Food, drink and tobacco
Textile goods and footware
Furniture
Medical equipment
Pharmaceuticals

**The top export partners:**
1. Germany
2. Italy
3. Croatia
4. France
5. Bosnia and Herzegovina
6. Yugoslavia
7. Poland
8. The Russian Federation
9. Great Britain
10. USA
11. Hungary
12. The Netherlands
13. The Czeck Republic
14. Switzerland
15. Slovakia
16. Macedonia
17. Spain
18. Denmark
19. Sweden

# What ethnic communities are there in Slovenia?

The total number of inhabitants: 1,976,290
87% of the total are Slovenes.

### Ethnic communities
The Italian ethnic community in the coastal region and the Hungarian in the eastern region of Prekmurje are autochthonous minority groups.

**Other ethnic groups**
came to Slovenia after the
World War II as labour
immigrants:

Croats
Serbs
Bosnians
Yugoslavs
Macedonians
Montenegrins
Albanians

# What religions are there in Slovenia?

The majority of the population
conforms to the Roman
Catholic Church and you will
find that a church tops almost
every hill.
Nonetheless, there are 30
registred religious communities
in Slovenia.

# Where are Slovenes in the world?

There are autochthonous Slovene minority groups living in Italy, Austria and Hungary. The number of Slovenes (depending on whether we consider the second and subsequent generations) living elswhere in the world but mostly in overseas (USA, Canada, Argentina, Australia) and EU countries ranges from 250,000 to 500,000.

### Slovenes in Austria
Present day Austrian **Carinthia** is the cradle of Slovenes. It is there that the first Slovene state was founded. Only a hundred years ago more Slovene newspapers were published in Klagenfurt, Austria, than in the Slovene capital, Ljubljana. One can still find Slovene place names there, although they bear official Austrian names now.
Most of the territory inhabited by Slovenes in the Austrian Carinthia lies in the Klagenfurt basin and its surroundings. Most Slovenes are situated in the valleys Zilja (the Gailtal), Rož (the Rosental), Podjuna (the Jauntal) and in the Glina area.
Some primary schools from these parts teach bilingual classes, i.e. German and Slovene, and there is a Slovene grammar school in Klagenfurt.

Present day Austrian **Styria** is yet another home to Slovenes but they are not officially recognized as a minority there.

The Slovene community in Austrian Carinthia is represented by the National Council of Slovenes in Carinthia, the Union of Slovene Organisations and Joint Coordinating Committee of Carinthian Slovenes; in Styria there is an active Cultural Association Article 7.

### Slovenes in Hungary
In Hungary, the Slovene minority mostly resides in the Porabje region; there is an active Union of Slovenes in Hungary where.
The Raba Slovenes are managed by local self-administration forms called *županija* in Železna (Vas Megye) and Zala (Zala Megye) respectively. Their cultural center is, however, in Monošter (Szengotthárd).
At first Slovenes populated a large part of the Pannonian Plain, where they founded an early medieval state, Lower Pannonia, with its seat near Lake Balaton.
On the arrival of Hungarians at the end of the 9th century, the area inhabited by Slovenes grew substantially smaller. Today Slovene settlements have managed to preserve themselves only in the most barren and remote parts of the Raba river basin.

## Slovenes in Italy

In Italy, Slovenes populate the Trst (Trieste), Gorica (Gorizia) and Videm (Udine) areas, and are organized in two umbrella organisations: the Slovene Cultural and Economic Union and the Council of Slovene Organisations.

**Valcanale Slovenes** live in the valley of Kanalska dolina (Valcanale) stretching from the West Julian Alps to the Karn Alps. They predominantly populate its central and eastern part, which is also ethnically mixed (Italians, Austrians, Slovenes). Some of the villages are Ukve, Ovčja vas, Žabnice ... The Slovene language is not officially recognized.

**Val Resia Slovenes** live in the single parallel valley in the Italian West Julian Alps – the Val Resia. This poorly connected, isolated valley under the mountain Kanin has managed to preserve its characteristic dialect and typical folk customs, which kindle the interest of ethnologists from all corners of the world.

**The Venetian Slovenes** inhabit the hilly district in which numerous valleys have been carved in by streams. These hills border on the Friuli plain, along which the ethnic border between the Friulians and Slovenes runs. This border has remained almost the same since the 6th century.

**Slovenes in the Goriško region** inhabit a stretch of land running along the state border between the hills Goriška Brda and the Adriatic Sea, which widens in the area of the Doberdob karst. Here on the edge of the plateau runs an ancient ethnic border.

**Slovenes** living in **Trst** (Trieste) and its hinterland enjoy the most rights among Slovene minorities in Italy. Together they persevere in their struggle for a uniform protection of the Slovene minority in Italy, governed by law.

The city of Trst (Trieste), which came to existence in the Middle Ages, prospered quickly on account of the Austrian seaport and the Vienna-Trieste rail connection. After World War I the city was assigned to Italy. Some years later, after World War II, this became a so called *free Trieste territory* and was divided into zones A and B respectively. It remained as such until 1954 when the London Memorandum assigned the former zone to Italy and the latter (the Slovene Littoral) to the then Yugoslavia.

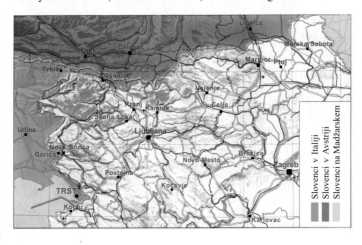

## What is the
## Slovene coat-of-arms like?

The Slovene coat-of-arms is in the form of a shield. The shield bears a central image of Mt. Triglav in white on a blue background. Two undulating blue lines below it represent the sea and rivers, and three six-pointed gold stars are arranged above in an inverted triangle.
The sides of the shield have a red border. The coat-of-arms is designed according to a particular geometric and colour scheme.

# What are the coats-of-arms of Slovene towns like?

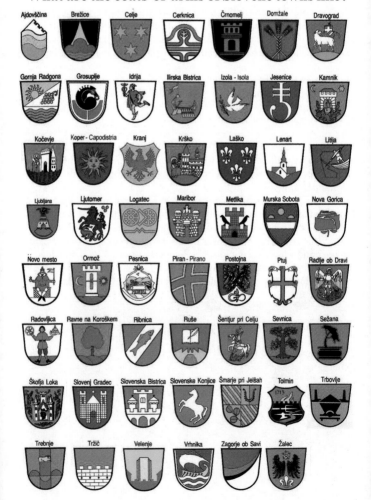

# What is the Slovene flag like?

The flag of the Republic of Slovenia consists of the popular tricolor (white-blue-red) plus the Slovene coat-of-arms. The proportion between the width and the length is 1 : 2. The white-blue-red combination appears in that order from top to bottom in three equal bands. The coat-of-arms is in the top left corner of the flag. One half of it reaches in the white band,

the other in the blue one.

# What is the Slovene national anthem like?

The text of the Slovene national anthem is the seventh stanza of a Toast (Zdravljica) by France Prešeren. The tune is taken from the choral work of the same name by the composer Stanko Premrl.

*Let's drink that every nation*
*Will live to see that bright day's birth*
*When neath the sun's rotation*
*Discent is banished from the earth,*
*Kill will be*
*Kinfolk free*
*With neighbeurs none in enemity*

# Customs and Tradition

# What is celebrated in Slovenia?

**Public holidays**
1st and 2nd January – New Year
8th February – Slovene Cultural Holiday; 27th
April –Day of Uprising Against Occupation;
1st and 2nd May – Labour Day
25th June – National Day
1st November – All Souls' Day; 26th
December – Independence Day

**Work-free days**
Easter Sunday and Easter Monday, Easter,
Whit Sunday, Whitsuntide
15th August – Assumption Day; 31th October
– Reformation Day; 25th December - Christmas

## New Year, 1st and 2nd January

On this day Slovenes like other nations of the world celebrate the parting
of the old and the beginning of a new year. Merry making and celebrations
start as early as the first half of December and reach their peak on New
Year's Eve on the 31st December. Many Slovenes celebrate it in the
streets. Such celebrations are organized in all big Slovene towns.

Father Frost brings presents on the last days of the old year and on the
first day of the new year. Needless to say, it is the children of Slovenia
who are most enthusiastic about this tradition!

Father Frost brings presents to
children in the cave Dimnice.

## Slovene Cultural Holiday, 8th February

On this day in 1849, France Prešeren, Slovenia's greatest poet, died in Kranj. To honour him Slovenes chose this day to be their cultural day.

## Easter

Long before the arrival of Christianity, Slovenes celebrated the victory of kind, spring spirits over winter demons. Though Christian religion has somewhat altered these celebrations many original features have still managed to survive.

Preparations for the Easter holiday start well before Easter Sunday. On Ash Wednesday a 40 day fasting period or Lent begins and lasts till Easter. But these days only a few still observe it. On Passion Sunday the cross is usually covered and on Palm Sunday colourful *butarice* made of coloured wooden carvings are brought to church. Once people believed *butarice* would protect them from storm and hail.

On Easter Saturday churchbells from every hill and valley start to chime and everybody rushes to mass and *žegen*. The young and old carry woven baskets or bags quaintly covered with small, embroidered tablecloths. Hiding shyly beneath are coloured eggs and cooked ham. Once the priest has blessed the food the feast can start - but not before the day is sloses. The fasting period is then over.

Depending on the region *pirhi* or coloured eggs can be adorned in various ways. Typically, in some parts of Slovenia eggs are coloured whereas in other parts patterns or decorations are scratched on them with a small knife. The most famous coloured eggs are the Bela Krajina (White Carniola) *pisanice*. In some places onion skins and other natural pigments are still used despite prevailing industrial colours and artificial decorations.

Pisanice from the Bela Krajina

## Day of Uprising Against Occupation, 27th April

On 27th April 1941, representatives of the Communists, Christian Socialists, democratic Sokoli (Falcons) and members of progressive Slovene culture gathered to set up the Liberation Front. This was an anti-fascist coalition and supreme Slovene authority that led organized resistance against the opressor during World War II. Hence this day is justifiably celebrated for those who fought and organized against the opressor.

## Labour Day, 1st and 2nd May

is another holiday that originates from pre-Christian times. On the eve of the the 1st May, Slovene villages like to compete to see which will set up the most beautiful *mlaj* or a maypole. This, however, is not only a Slovene tradition as maypoles can be seen in many other European countries on this day. In some countries a maypole can be a peeled spruce or pine tree, a poplar or even a birch.

In 1889, May 1st was declared an international holiday at the 1st Congress of the Second International *in memoriam* of bloody events, which had occured in Chicago in 1886. At that time the US police killed or wounded more than 200 picketers who demanded an eight-hour work day. Many a Slovene pins a red or white carnation in the buttonhole on May 1st. The night before this holiday bonfires are lit across the country to remind us of the Turks who used to loot Slovene territory for two centuries. When there was an imminent Turk danger, Slovene ancestors lit bonfires as a signal.

## National Day, 25th June

Because of deepening antagonism within Yugolavia between nationalities and in other respects, a referendum was held in Slovenia on December 23rd, 1990. The turnout was 93.2% and 88,2% votes were cast "for" a sovereign and independent state of Slovenia. This act of popular self-determination laid the basis for Slovenia's national independence.

This action was followed by a ten-day war in which the Yugoslav army failed to prevent Slovenia from gaining independence!

## Reformation Day, 31st October

Primož Trubar (1508 - 1586) undoubtedly marks the birth of Slovene literature. His works, on which the Protestant movement was based in Slovenia, clearly demonstrate that this nation was an equal member in a group of other cultivated European nations. Primož Trubar's importance in the history of the Slovene nation is priceless. He published 24 books, 22 of which were in Slovene and 2 in German. The first, the Alphabet Book, came out as early as 1551. Thus Slovenes did not get their first book by coincidence like most European nations. Slovene Protestants of the time were overwhelmed by their desire and need to develop the Slovene written language and begin a literary tradition. Consequently, Reformation Day is not only celebrated by Slovene Protestants but Slovenes in general. The Bohorič grammar, the Megiser Slovene-Latin-German Dictionary and Dalmatin's translation of the Bible are more proof that their work was not coincidental.

# How do Slovenes celebrate folk festivities?

## Gregorjevo, 12th March

Gregorjevo is the first day of spring. It is the day when "birds get married."

On this day a bear comes out of its den and feels a willow twig. If it is pliable, the bear slouches off to run its spring errands and if it is not, it returns inside to sleep.

Not only does Gregor mark the beginning of the spring, he also makes days longer. Indispensible candlelight, which blacksmiths and shoemakers needed during the day, thus became redundant so they gathered the night before Gregorjevo and threw the lamps into the water.

This old custom is still revived in the towns of Tržič, Kropa and Železniki where children make small houses and ships of all shapes and sizes, cover their windows with colourful transparencies and put a candle inside. The night before Gregorjevo their masterpieces are brought to local rivers and launched.

## Jurjevo, 24th April

In ancient times this was a great folk festival. Every year, Slovene forefathers were visited by old Vestnik, the god of spring. Upon the arrival of Christianity the old, peaceful Vestnik was defeated in a bloody battle by St. Jurij (St. George), who took his place. Even today Slovenes like to celebrate the victory of spring over winter. This custom is specially observed in the Bela Krajina but also elsewhere in the country where Zeleni Jurij (green George) is greeted according to old customs.

## Kresovanje, 24th June

The fear of the sun dying is one of the oldest fears of men. The Slovene forefathers used to thank the sun for its help by lighting bonfires on high hills where they were closest to the sun. It was this magical power of the fire that was to help the sun to shine forever and never die away.

Not only did this magical power of fire make fields fertile, it also kept people healthy. Jumping over a bonfire was a part of the ritual as the fire purified and bestowed health upon people.

Kresovanje or Ivanje celebrates the arrival of the summer though the season itself commences a few days earlier according to the calendar. The night from the 23rd to 24th June was the time when Slovene forefathers worshiped Kresnik, the son of the sun deity Svetovid. The Church replaced him with Janez Krstnik i.e. John the Baptist. Since both names Kresnik and Krstnik are quite similar Janez (John) became the most common name in Slovenia and "kranjski Janez" or "Carniolan John" a synonym for a Slovene.

## What are the Slovene national flowers?

Due to diverse countryside and climate conditions we cannot speak of only one national flower. The carnation from the Gorenjsko region is surely one and though it is not indigenous to Slovenia it can be seen from most galleries or "ganki" in Gorenjsko. A geranium of the pelargonium family, which originates from Africa, was adopted by Slovenes as their own and in the Slovene Littoral a rosemary is considered as a national flower.

# Martinovo (Martinmas), 11. november

During their autum festivities Slovene ancestors thanked their gods for bountiful crops and prayed for their good favour in times to come. Their forefathers' spirits regularly came to visit them as well.

Even today when crops are harvested, wine stored and pastures grazed, Slovenes like to mark the end of autumn farming by treating themselves to a sumptuous feast.

Different parts of Slovenia observe Martinovo or autumn Shrovetide by giving a typical and traditional culinary feast. Tables weaken under the load of delicious dishes, which show how fine the crops were. And Martinovo is incomplete without Martin's goose! This was sacrificed in old times and there are numerous supertstitions about it.

Fortunetelling is still common at every Martin's feast: "If the goose's breast bone is brown, a cold winter is to come. Should the bone be white, lots of snow will be in sight ... "

A goose is related to the story of St. Martin as well: when they searched for him to ordain him as bishop, this humble saint had hid himself among a flock of geese.

St. Martin has a special power, namely to turn water into wine. Thus this festivity is most solemn in wine growing regions of Slovenia. On Martin's Day must turns into wine. This calls for raising your glasses and saying:

"Here comes, here comes Martin the saint,
he blessed the wine, I'll drink it."

When the feast is over, there has to be a brimming majolica and some food left on the table for the spirits of our forefathers, who come for a visit.

## St. Nicholas' Day, 5th December

For centuries the Catholic Church fruitlessly prosecuted wild winter merrymakings of masked people dressed like demons and the spirits of their forefathers, in an attempt to make them more christian. The visits of St. Nicholas and his accompanying devils – parkeljni - thus became a Christian tradition.

Children still believe that St. Nicholas holds two books in his hands: a golden one and a black one. Since St. Nicholas knows and sees everything, he meticulously notes down children's good and bad deeds in his two books. On the eve of the event it is thus important to place some straw baskets or bowls for the saint to fill them with goodies such as sweets and dried or fresh fruit.

## What is the difference between a Loka and Dražgoše small bread?

A small bread, a Loka bread or even a honey bread are but a few names used to describe honey pastry made of rye or white flour, honey, pepper, cinnamon, carnation cloves and potash.

The dough for this small bread is shaped in two different ways. The Loka bread is impressed in baking molds, whereas the Dražgoše bread is shaped manually.

In the town of Škofja Loka the bread was shaped in molds only, in the valleys of Poljanska and Selška dolina, however, both ways were applied.

## Where can I find
## Slovene folk songs and folk music?

You can find a great archive of Slovene folk songs and folk music at the following website: http://www.zrc-sazu.si/gni/ It is archived, maintained and complemented by: Glasbenonarodopisni inštitut (Institute of Ethnomusicology SRC SASA) ZRC SAZU Gosposka 13 1000 Ljubljana

## What are beehives?

For a Slovene a bee is a model of dilligence and a symbol of fertility. Apiculture has a long tradition in Slovenia. In the 18th and 19th century the rearing of honeybees was an important branch of farming. Due to its long tradition, the introduction of beehives and the autochtonous Carniolan bee (apis mellifera carnica) apiculture became famous in Europe and a Slovene beekeeper, Anton Janša (1734-1773), was named the head beekeeper to the court of the Hapsburg empress Maria Teresia.

Simultaneously a remarkable art of painting these beehives evolved, which is one of the most original Slovene economic-cultural traditions that cannot be found anywhere in the world!

These beehives show many motifs originating from folk tradition, religion and history, folk fables, humour ...

## Are Slovenes gullible?

Several superstitions and beliefs date back to pre-Christian times. Witches and demons were at their worst behaviour during long winter nights and to keep safe from them a lot of farmers still place a dungfork, rake or harrow with its spikelike teeth facing out beside their cowshed door. This way a witch cannot enter the cowshed and stir up the cattle. Such a trapping device turned out to be fatal for many a witch.

Should Slovenes meet a chimneysweep, they will still grasp a button and release it when they come across a white horse. But horse teams have not been seen for decades now and white cars are everywhere!
If a black cat crosses the street in front of you, this is a bad omen. Or walking under a ladder – this is believed to bring bad luck. Or the number 13 – not very popular as you can imagine.

## Are Slovenes envious?

Slovenes are ordinary people. They say they persist in this world just to see how others will break their necks and often find pleasure in other people's failure.

Never mind, thinks a Slovene to himself, if my calf drops dead. As long as my neighbour's cow dies too.

But it is also true that Slovenes are well aware of the mistakes they make. And it is rightly so! If not, how could they ascribe them to others?
If you are staying in Slovenia for a short time, you won't notice this because, all in all, Slovenes are friendly and hospitable people.

## Are Slovenes belligerent?

History does not record any armed attacks made by Slovenes. They were always victims of other oppressors and though the enemy had always managed to oppress them it failed to defeat them! One glance at Slovene history reveals the downfall of the Frankish Empire, Avars are long gone, the Holy Roman Empire crumbled, the Turks were driven away, Napoleon was defeated, Austria-Hungary and Yugoslavia disintegrated. Nonetheless Slovenes persevere despite the fact that they do not have an army, a strong state or developed economy.

In spite of its turbulent history this nation has managed to continue steadfastly in this strategically important part of Europe where routes from east to west and north to south intersect. Slovenes chose culture and art, language and folk songs over arms to be their shield and grew into a nation of poets. If the history of other nations was as peaceful as this one, the world would be a much better place to live in.

## Do Slovenes like to sing?

Slovenes are a nation of singers. Choral singing is so popular that every village has its own choir or at least an octet or a quartet if there are not enough people.
These numerous choirs keep up rich the tradition of Slovene folk singing. Their repertoire also includes very demanding chamber music choral compositions. The quality of a great number of these choirs is such that they have achieved international fame and are repeatedly awarded with prizes.

# Free time, food and drinks

# What do Slovenes like to eat?

Slovene cuisine is as diverse as it is its landscape and some old national dishes, which cherish a rich tradition, have managed to preserve themselves throughout the centuries till today. Slovenia is divided into approximately 40 culinary regions. Besides different eating habits these regions are characterized by their typical dishes. A different ground structure and varying climate as well as economic and cultural factors have contributed their part in tailoring this nation's diet.

The menu in Slovene kitchens consists of exquisite and rich dishes once prepared by nobility, a wide variety of town dishes, culinary treats of simple farm food and dishes that used to be typical of miners from Idrija, rafters from the valley of Savinjska dolina, lumberjacks, parish priests and many more.

Slovene cuisine of today consists mainly of simple home-made dishes prepared in an inventive and imaginative way. Dishes that were once laid on a farmer's table on special occasions are still a true feast today.

As a nation of bread eaters Slovenes consider bread very important. There is practically no meal without bread. The tradition of home-made bread is truly an old one. The day a housewife kneaded dough and baked it in the farm stove was a feast in the Slovene countriside. But bread was not baked every day. The housewife usually made a week's provision. Many housewives in the rural parts of Slovenia still bake bread to last a week or longer and there is no industrially baked bread that would be as tasty as the one from a farm stove. Any visitor to Slovenia can see this for himself should he stay at any of the numerous tourist farmhouses where genuine home made food and wine are still served.

# What are koline?

The day a butcher comes to your home is a joyful one even if the family have to roll up their sleeves more than usual. Typically, a butcher would come early in the morning accompanied by neighbours. They would lend him a helping hand and tie the pig.

The pig is the king among animals in Slovenia and pork meat a main dish in most Slovene homes even today. The koline or the annual killing of a pig is the biggest winter holiday in the Slovene countryside. Lavish meals, home-made dishes, numerous folk ways and customs mark this event. On such a day it is customary to bring some of the sausages or meat to your neighbour as a token of good will.

Blood sausages are well-known in all parts of Slovenia. They are a dark sausage with a mixture of blood, entrails, millet and buckwheat porridge. Neighbours often bring these to each other as a gift.

The most common pork meat specialty is a sausage. However, if you want to try something better, we suggest ham or smoked pork leg joint. This is known in all Slovenia.

The Primorsko region is famous for its prosciutto or pork leg joint cured by drying. Furthermore, stuffed pork stomach is another typical product, the preparation of which is particular to region. Some prefer it smoked, others dried...

# Is Slovenia a wine-growing country?

Slovenia has always been a home to the vine, as its wine growing regions run along the 40.5° and 46.5° parallel north, which is the typical latitude of other European wine regions i.e. the renowned Burgundy and Bordeaux regions in France.

Despite the fact that its 21,000 ha of vineyards rank Slovenia among the world's minor wine producers on a world scale, wine producing and wine trade have always constituted an important part of Slovene culture and tradition. The collection of wines is rich and their numerous international prizes speak of their quality.

Due to the wine's protected geographical origin and varying climate conditions Slovenia falls into three wine growing regions:

"No flower in the world
can match the beauty of this vine."
Bishop A. M. Slomšek

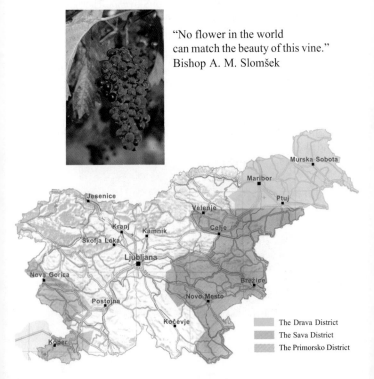

The Drava District
The Sava District
The Primorsko District

## Where can I get spirits?

Spirits can be obtained in almost any bar, pub or restaurant and in all retail markets selling food.

One look at the shelves shows a wide choice of drinks. You can get practically anything: from beer of different producers, quality Slovene wines to spirits of all brands.

## Where is the oldest vine?

"The old vine" is the pride and symbol of both Maribor and the wine growing regions of Slovenia. You can find it in the central part of the old town, in Lent by the river Drava. The old vine has grown there for more than four centuries and is one of the oldest indigenous vintage types of grape in Slovenia. It is called modra kavčina, žametna črnina or žametovka (a kind of dark grape).

# Do Slovenes have drinking problems?

People have known alcohol for thousands of years. Since ancient times philosophers have written about it and poets celebrated it in their verse. Its literary references date back to the Old and New Testament. For centuries alcohol has played an important part in religion, medical science and culture and today alcohol can be obtained in most countries worldwide. People are well disposed to it and countries make profits from its production and consumption.

Nevertheless, drinking alcohol can be hazardous. Many tragedies and sufferings have been caused by it and those affected are not only its consumers but also innocent victims.

Still, Slovenes like to hit the bottle, as they say. No wonder: singing and drinking go hand in hand. The Slovene national anthem starts like this:

> Anew the wines have fruited
> And borne us, my good friends sweet wine
> To charge our blood diluted,
> To clear our heart, our eye define,
> To suppress
> All distress
> And waken hope in saddened brest.

## How do Slovenes spend their free time?

This nation likes to travel. The favourite free-time activity is spending some time in natural surroundings and whatever direction you may head in you can easily make a short trip there. That's Slovenia.

The history of mountain climbing is more than 200 years old and there are more than 100,000 Slovenes who are affiliated members of mountain societies and you can find many more on well marked and explained mountain trails. It is therefore no coincidence that a branched network of well marked trails and supplied mountain huts was set up in highlands and on foothills.

Slovenes like to sing in choirs and participate in other cultural activities. Almost any village prides itself on their cultural and artistic society or a theatre group and each new local performance by their amateur actors is greeted with enthusiasm.

Slovenes do not only see the beauties of their own country. This is a nation of keen, curious and eager travellers who are thirsty for knowledge so do not be surprised if you meet one in a most distant part of the world.

# What makes Slovenes laugh?

"Every nation makes fun of their neighbours and everybody is right!" Those were the words of a German philosopher, A. Schopenhauer, and most European nations are guilty of this. Just think what the English say about the French, the Germans about the Czechs, The French about the Germans ...

However European the Slovene nation may be it is somewhat different from other nations in this respect. They primarily make fun of themselves and their own fate and draw strength from it. This is how they have managed to survive on this small piece of the European puzzle. And despite constant external efforts to supress and oppress them no one has ever managed to defeat them.

## Two jokes
### On grief

Our heavenly father descends to Earth to perform good deeds and comes across a weeping man by the side of the road.
"Pray, good man, why do you weep? Tell me your reason and I'll help you," says the Lord to him.
"I'm doomed and not even our Lord can help me," retorts the man.
"Where is the reason for your grief?" asks the Lord again.
The man looks at him and says:
"I'm Slovene!"
Upon hearing these words even the Lord is overwhelmed with tears and sets off again on his way.
(Taken from the anecdote by the Slovene playwright and writer, Ivan Cankar (1876 - 1918).

## On stinginess

On a hot Sunday afternoon in summer an exhausted climber reaches the first farmhouse on the outskirts of a mountain village. After hiking for three days and spending two nights sleeping on and under a table in two overcrowded huts the climber is so thirsty that his tongue sticks to the roof of his mouth. There is nothing he would like better than a beer or two but to quench his thirst he would not say no to the clear spring water he sees running along a carved wooden gutter into a long wooden trough. Upon spotting this from the top of the meadow, the climber heads towards the trough.

The water murmurs temptingly and an old woman fiddles around the trough.

"Good day to you, old lady," says the climber, his voice husky and dry.

" Good day," says the woman not even raising an eyebrow. She has already taken a good look at him as he was coming across the meadow but he was of no interest to her.

"I've just  been to the mountains and I'm so thirsty. Can I have some water?"

"Go and ask my neighbour, his water is cooler," says the old woman briskly and continues her pursuit.

# Geographical characteristics

## What four geographical units meet in Slovenia?

In Slovenia four large European relief units meet: the Alps, the Dinaric Mountains, the Mediterranean basin and the Pannonian Plain. Moreover, the country, which lies in the contact zone of two immense litospheric plates - the African and Eurazian respectively - can be divided in eight more or less completed geographical regions: Primorsko, Notranjsko, Gorenjsko, Dolenjsko, Bela krajina, Koroško, Štajersko and Prekmurje.

The diverse geological structure, uneven relief (from the sea level to the height of 2864 m) and four biogeographical areas that Slovenia covers are projected in the rich flora and fauna. Besides 3,000 ferns and flowering plants and 50,000 different animal species there are also numerous endimic animals and plants.

# Where is the lowest natural pass from Central Europe to the Mediterranean basin?

The Postojna Gate if we can call it so due to its mere 612 m height above sea level has always been an important passage. Ancient Argonauts used this convenient natural pass to transport their ship from the Sava to the sea. Throughout known history an important road connection led through Postojna and it still does. This is the only connection between the Slovene capital and the coast.

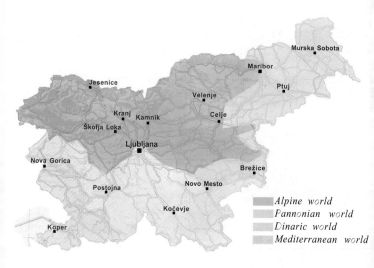

# Where do the Alps start in Europe?

The Alps, a European mountain arc, begin or end in Slovenia... depending on your perspective. The easternmost part of the Alps ends with the Julian Alps, the Karavanke mountain range and the Kamnik Alps. Moreover, almost a third of Slovenia's territory is covered in Alpine foothills. Slovenes like to say they live "on the sunny side of the Alps".

# What is the weather in Slovenia like?

In Slovenia the climate can be narrowed down to three prevailing types: Alpine, Continental and Mediterranean.

The lowest temperature ever (-26°C) was measured at Kredarica in the 1991-2000 period and the highest (38°C) in Črnomelj.

At Kredarica there were as many as 237 cold days with temperature below zero, in Rateče the respective number was 149 and in Slovenj Gradec 125.

The number of warm days with a temperature above 25°C was 97 in Portorož, 96 in Vipava and 93 in Bilje.

| town | January | June | precipitation v mm |
|------|---------|------|--------------------|
| Celje | 0.3 | 20.2 | 1,119 |
| Ljubljana | 0.8 | 21.0 | 1,352 |
| Maribor | 0.4 | 20.8 | 1,044 |
| Murska Sobota | - 0.4 | 20.5 | 806 |
| Novo Mesto | 0.4 | 20.5 | 1,161 |
| Portorož | 4.8 | 22.5 | 934 |
| Slap pri Vipavi | 3.7 | 21.3 | 1,554 |
| Bovec | - 3.0 | 19.2 | 2,634 |
| Letališče Brnik | - 0.8 | 19.2 | 1,320 |
| Črnomelj | 0.7 | 21.1 | 1,277 |
| Ilirska Bistrica | 1.7 | 19.8 | 1,267 |
| Kočevje | - 0.5 | 18.4 | 1,460 |
| Kredarica | - 6.1 | 6.5 | 2,032 |
| Lesce | - 1.2 | 18.7 | 1,504 |
| Postojna | 0.3 | 18.4 | 1,611 |
| Rateče-Planica | - 3.3 | 16.7 | 1,449 |
| Slovenj Gradec | - 1,.9 | 18.4 | 1,217 |
| Velenje | 0.6 | 19.7 | 1,121 |
| Bilje | 3.5 | 22.2 | 1,566 |

Average annual temperature and precipitation level in Slovenia in the 1991-2000 period.

# What is the Karst?

The world stretched between the mountain Triglav, the Adriatic Sea and the river Kolpa hides in its bosom an underground kingdom, hidden from the eyes of local people and visitors. This is a complex labyrinth of precipices, caves, tunnels and streams. Through millions of sinkholes water disappears underground. Thousands of precipices, some truly gigantic, are cleft in the crust. Rivers, forming magnificent waterfalls, numerous rapids and lakes, run in the underground through unknown and partly explored underground gorges. This is a spectacular world, mostly in parts where big galleries have been formed in soluble limestone by the action of water. In this complete darkness millions of stalactites and stalagmites have been formed. A rare visitor to this strange world stands in awe of their amazing colours and shapes if he sees them lit for a brief moment.

Speleology has quite a tradition in Slovenia. The Speleological Association of Slovenia was founded as early as 1889 and consists of 50 speleological societies and clubs.

Foreigners have come across **the Slovene word *kras*** in the Slovene region the Kras. The word has been accepted worldwide in its original or somewhat adapted form (karst, carso) and denotes karst phenomena, which are the same or similar to those in Slovenia. As much as 44% of the Slovene territory is of karst structure and 8,000 underground caves and precipices have been explored so far.

## Where are seasonal lakes?

The Notranjsko region is unique in the world. Underground rivers resurface every now and then to roar their brief song to the sun and quickly disappear the darkness of the underground. Spring and autumn rains fill remarkable seasonal lakes, true pearls of unspoilt nature.

The vast grassland of the Cerknica polje gets submerged as well and fills a lake that measures up to 24 km$^2$. When the water flows away, streams meander across the grassland and a myriad of sinkholes that conduct water to the underground become apparent.

The water from the lake resurfaces in the depression Rakov Škocjan, runs for a mere 2 km and disappears again underground.
After that the stream runs through dark passages of the cave Planinska jama and flows into the river Pivka, which runs through the Postojna Cave.

The confluence on this river is called Unica and it gushes in the Planina polje. This too gets submerged if it rains heavily.
On the other side of the polje the Unica sinks again and resurfaces at Vrhnika as the river Ljubljanica.

1. Lake Cerknica
2. the Planinsko polje
3. seasonal lakes in the vicinity of Pivka
4. the Radna polje

river basin:
—— the Ljubljanica
—— underground flow

# Which caves are open to tourists?

There are as many as 8,000 explored underground caves and precipices in Slovenia but only 23 are open to tourists. The company of these strange underground caves got richer for underground tunnels of a former mercury mine in Idrija. In Velenje tunnels are used for a museum presentation on coal mining. In Mežica and in the mountain Peca lead and zinc mines have been brought to life.

the cave Sveta jama

**Caves open to tourists**
1. the Dimnice in the Matarsko podolje (system of valleys)
2. the Divača cave
3. the cave Francetova jama
4. the caves Gabrovška jama-Frežnarjeva jama
5. the cave under the cliff Babji zob
6. the cave under the Predjama Castle
7. the Kostanjevica cave
8. the cave Križna jama
9. Pekel in the Savinja valley
10. the Pivka and the cave Črna jama
11. the cave Planinska jama
12. the Postojna Cave
13. the cave Ravenska jama
14. the cave Rotovnikova jama
15. the cave Snežna jama on the mountain Raduha
16. the Škocjan Caves
17. the cave Sveta jama near Socerb
18. a great icy cave in Paradana
19. the cave Vilenica
20. the caves Zadlaška jama - Dantejeva jama
21. the caves Zelške jame
22. the cave Železna jama near Gorjuša
23. the caves Županova jama - Taborska jama

The cave Županova jama

**Mines**
24. Antonijev rov (Anthony mine shaft) - Idrija Mercury Mine
25. Velenje Coal Mine
26. Mežica Lead Mine

# Is there a cave dragon in Slovenia?

High waters from karst caves in Notranjsko have often washed ashore "dragon's young" as it was once believed. Thus people thought underground caves were a home to a live dragon. The first scientific description of this unusual animal dates back in 1768.

Due to the colour of its skin the animal was named the human fish or proteus. It can grow 30 cm long and live for more than 100 years. It is the only cave vertebrate in Europe and the biggest cave animal in the world.

The proteus (proteus anguinus) has long been a symbol of the classical or original karst and a national symbol. It dwells in inaccessible water tunnels and underground lakes of the deep karst. It is still an unresolved mystery how it manages to survive in complete darkness.

More proof of that is a black proteus was found as recently as 1986, which was also washed ashore. It lives in Bela Krajina in an area of a mere 50 km². Besides differing in colour both proteuses differ phisically. The black one has eyes whereas the white one does not. Its eyes are stunted.

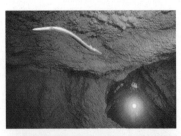

# Why are the Škocjan Caves so special?

Karst has been explored since antiquity and the Škocjan Caves kindled interest even then. The place where the river Reka mysteriously disappears underground has fueled people's imagination till the present day. We also come across the Reka river over 200 m underground in the cave Kačna jama near Divača. After that the Reka disapppears into the mysterious underground and resurfaces again as the Timav in the Gulf of Trieste.

The Škocjan Caves are also special due to the size of their underground galleries. The Martel gallery is 250 m long, 120 m wide and 140 m high. By 1904 the whole system of the Škocjan Caves had been explored. Local people have built kilometres of paths along vertical and overhanging walls of the underground tunnels. They have cut the path in bedrock and sinter, secured it with iron wedges and wires to cling to, and built wooden footbridges and small bridges. Some paths lead just under the roof of the cave, 90 m high above the foamy and roaring Reka.

# What are
# Slovene forests like?

More than half of Slovenia is woodland (62%) and only Finland and Sweden outrank it in Europe. No wonder Slovenes like to go for a walk in the near-by forest. Typically, to get some fresh air, pick mushrooms and fruits.

Beech is a foster mother to all Slovene forests. It grows in the forests stretching from the Pannonian Plain to the upper forest limit in the Alps.

Nevertheless, a Slovene forest is not only beech. It is thousands of various plant and animal species. 50 forest paths laid down for educational purposes teach about this ecosystem, which is getting a lot of attention all over the country. Still, only a handfull can truly grasp this unique creation of nature.

**The Rajhenav virgin forest** at the height of 870 - 920 m above sea level in the heart of the Kočevski Rog measures 51 ha and consists of fir and beech.

## Tree giants
- the Najevnik linden on the peak Lundranski vrh above Črna na
  Koroškem – tunk circumference: 11 m;
- the Kovačič oak in Gregovci near Brežice - circumference: 7.5 m;
- the Zajčar chestnut in Florjanu above Zminc in the in the valley
  Poljanska dolina - 10 m;
- the Marolt fir in the valley Globoka dolina by the stream Bistriški potok
  on the Pohorje - circumference: 6 m;
- the biggest larch grows in Mala Pišnica under the Grlo at the height of
  1460 m above sea level - circumference: 4 m;
- the Jurše yew tree in Log near Ruše - circumference: 4.3 m;
- "by three spruces" on the plateau Trnovski gozd - circumference: 5.8 m;
- the almost 60 m high Zgorn spruce on the Pohorje is considered the
  highest tree in Slovenia;

# Tourist information and locations

# How many people have been to the Postojna Cave?

The Postojna Cave is a 22 km long system of underground tunnels and galleries. It is the biggest cave on the classic karst and the longest Slovene cave. Its entrance has long fired the imagination of its visitors. The first are known to have been there as early as the 13th century.

In the mid 17th century natural scientists first pursued their interest in the cave and it is here that speleology was born. Numerous new species of cave fauna have been found, among them the proteus. The speleobiological laboratory in the cave is still performing an important function.

There have been guided tours since 1818. From 1872 it was possible to see the cave from an electric train and in1884 the cave got its first electric light. So far almost 30 million visitors from all over the world have seen the Postojna Cave.

From the total of 5.2 km, which are open to public, 3.5 km can be seen from the train and 1.7 km on foot.

## Why do tourists visit the Predjama castle?

The Predjama Castle is undoubtedly the finest castle in Slovenia. It is literary perched amid a 123 m high rocky precipice and highly inaccessible to all intruders. It is impressive yet simple and its interesting tales and real treasures make it even more magnificent.

One of the most interesting tales is about a robber baron, Erazem Predjamski, who used his invincible castle to raid caravans of traders, the rich and, in particular, the clergy. Erazem did not steal only for himself but often distributed the loot among his poor subjects.

For a long time the imperial army made efforts to besiege the robber's nest but in vain. In the wintertime when the army's supplies were already running out Erazem mocked his enemy from the fortified walls and sent them roast oxen and other treats galore. On a Friday he would supply them with the most beautiful fresh fish and fresh fruit awaited them almost every day. No sooner had blossoms from cherry trees in Predjama withered away, that Erazem had already brought fresh cherries to his enemy. But how? Surely he could not have any more supplies in the besieged castle? As a result many believed Erazem had a true paradise in his cave.

Then the commander of the imperial army bribed Erazem's servant, who was bringing him messages and gifts from his master. It was he who let the enemy know when and where Erazem went "where even an emperor walks". And the cannons, which had waited for almost a year in the pasture, aimed at the castle and fired their stone cannonballs. They did not kill Erazem. He was buried under the rocks that broke off. These events were back in 1483.

The barron is buried near the church from the 15th century, which stands on a slope in front of the castle. A lime tree was planted there and many a visitor to Predjama rests in its cool shadow.

## Why is Bled so popular among tourists?

The solitary hills jutting from the plain and surrounding Lake Bled are typical of the Bled area. The glacial lake fills a basin in the middle of glacial rubble and has a reputation of being extremely picturesque. Its is adorned by the medieval castle perched on top of a high natural cliff-face and by an islet with a church. The shore has been turned into a magnificent park with villages, villas and hotels. In the background of this earthly paradise we can see the forest-covered slopes of Jelovica with its rocky edge, the cliff Babji zob and the Pokljuka plateau, above which the white peaks of the Julian Alps can be seen on clear days.

The poet France Prešeren (1800-1849) wrote these lines about Bled:
*Nowhere in the world is there a more lovely place,
than this paradise and its suroundings"*

# Where are thermal water springs and health spas?

The verified status of a natural health spa has been conferred to as many as 15 Slovene spas, two of which are found in the coastal region (Strunjan and Portorož) and the other 13 in the subpannonian belt. Here, at the meeting point of the Pannonian, Dinaric and Alpine world natural thermal and mineral water springs out.

The spas are popular tourist recreational centres.

Thermal water from these parts has been known since ancient times.

A specific microclimate, unspoilt nature and thermal water of different mineral content and temperature ($32^0$ to $73°C$) have led to both the development and establishment of Slovene health spas.

Europe has known and consumed Slovene mineral water (Radenska and Rogaška) for more than 400 years.

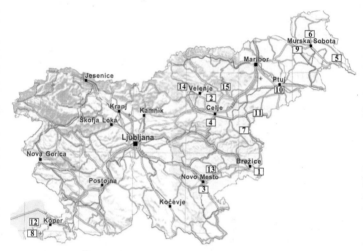

1. The spa **Terme Čatež** - "Slovene bathing riviera";
2. The thermal spa **Toplice Dobrna** – first recorded in 1147;
3. The health spa **Zdravilišče Dolenjske Toplice** – known since medieval times; The first building dates back in the 17th century;
4. The health spa **Zdravilišče Laško** – from the times of Roman legionaries; It flourished during the era of the Austrian emeperor Francis Joseph I.
5. The thermal spa **Terme Lendava** – while drilling for oil a thermal spring was found;
6. The health spa **Zdravilišče Moravske toplice** – their history is similar to that of Lendava;
7. The health spa **Zdravilišče Olimia**
8. The thermal spa **Terme Talasoterapija Portorož**
9. The health spa **Zdravilišče Radenci** – Radenska - Tri srca mineral water
10. The thermal spa **Terme Ptuj**
11. The health spa **Zdravilišče Rogaška** – many legends speak of its orgin. According to an ancient one, the winged horse, Pegasus, opened this magic spring of thermal water with a stroke of its hoof.
12. The health spa **Zdravilišče Strunjan**
13. The spa **Šmarješke toplice**
14. The thermal spa **Terme Topolšica** – the healing effects of thermal water were already known in the 16th century;
15. The health resort **Zreče-Rogla**

# Where are festivals held?

Almost any bigger Slovene town organizes a festival of some sort or a range of cultural and entertaining open-air events. There are, however, some festivals, which need to be pointed out:

**The Ljubljana Summer Festival,** which is the oldest Slovene festival, is the nation's premier cultural celebration held in Ljubljana. Lately, its name has been a synonym for performances made by prominent classical music virtuosos, host performances by orchestras, opera and ballet houses, ethno and jazz concerts, art exhibitions, a colony of artists, street performances and many more.

**Festival Lent** is a Maribor event. Though much shorter in time than the one in Ljubljana it is amazing to see the city during the festival.

**Festival Stična** is another event that deserves mentioning. An annual singing contest of Slovene choirs is held here and is attended by more than a hundred choirs.

## Where are carnivals?

On the first Sunday preceeding *pust* (Shrovetide) the town of Ptuj organizes a carnival. This is really an opening ceremony where traditional and carnival masks from Slovenia and abroad are presented. In the week to follow various merry events take place. They culminate on Shrove Sunday with a procession of masked people. *Kurenti* and other traditional Slovene folk figures revel till Shrove Tuesday.

All big Slovene towns organize traditional carnivals but they are no match for Ptuj. Here most masked people take part in the processions and the public simply have a good time.

Speaking of traditional masks one must mention carnivals held in Cerknica and Cerkno with their *cerkljanski laufarji*.

## What is a *kurent*?

The greatest attraction from the Ptuj Plain (Ptujsko polje) is a *kurent*, a creature from beyond. It is supposedly a symbol of spring and fertility, a caller of new life. But *kurent* is a creature of mystery. Nobody knows which ancient times it comes from and to what purpose.

## What is a Slovene inn like?

For ages, inns have been a firm part of the Slovene tradition. They were places where people gathered, talked and had fun. Big things happened in them... Many a Slovene still uses this pleasant environment for meetings and doing business.

In the last few decades a new boom from abroad caught up with Slovenia. Pizza places and fast food restaurants have sprung up everywhere. But a Slovene inn is different. It breathes architecture, it breathes culture. It returns to its origin, tradition and has much more to offer: a wide selection of national dishes, quality Slovene wine, a chat with friendly hosts. They are a part of the inventory. More or less, that is. Some less, some more ...

## What is a *veselica*?

In every village in Slovenia there is a voluntary fire department, which organizes a party or *veselica* at least once a year. They put up a makeshift platform made of spruce planks, bring some tables and benches and arrange them nicely in the meadow in the middle of the village. On the platform a band of musicians with an indispensable accordionist plays merry tunes and the air fills up with cheers, polkas and walzes. Local and near-by villagers attend such parties. There are sausages galore, barrels of beer and wine. Sometimes a bunch of provocative youngsters from near-by villages show their fists. A *veselica* usually starts in the middle of the day and lasts late in the night or quite often till morning.

## What is *osmica*?

The empress Maria Teresia (1717-1780) granted wine producers permission to sell wine surpluses of the previous year in a temporary open-air bar beneath a *frasko,* which is how this custom got its name. You see, bunches of ivy or *fraske,*which are hung over the main door, kindly invite you to *osmica.*

The tradition of *osmica* is still cherished in the Primorsko region in the valley Vipavska dolina, in Brda, in the vicinity of Nova Gorica, in the Kras as well as in the hinterland of Koper. But wine is not the only magnet for people. This custom would be unimaginable without delicious Primorsko dishes.

## Where can I get information about tourist events?

The Tourist Association of Slovenia, which was established in 1905, is a national, non-profit and non-governmental organisation independent of any party. This Association, which operates as an institution of civil society, unites more than 520
tourist societies, 23 municipal and regional associations as well as 58 tourist information centres. Besides other information their website includes also a calender of events in Slovenia.
You can find it at: http://www.turisticna-zveza.si

## Where can I obtain tourist information?

Slovene Tourist Organisatio or STO is a state institution which provides all the necessary information. Their website address is:
**http://www.slovenia-tourism.si**

# Where do I get information on customs regulations?

It is best to turn to Customs Administration of the Republic of Slovenia.
Their website address is:
http://www.sigov.si/mf/slov/curs/curs2.htm

# Where do I get rail information?

Any information regarding train timetables, passenger, goods and rail
traffic are included on the Internet page of the Slovenske železnice:
http://www.slo-zeleznice.si/

# Where can I get tickets for sport events and matches?

The widest selection of tickets can be obtained at the branch office of the
Kompas tourist agency in Slovenska cesta 36, Ljubljana.
Their e-mail address is: slovenska@kompas.si

## How do I find addresses of Slovene people?

Try the phone book of the Republic of Slovenia, which is also available on-line: http://tis.telekom.si/

## Where can I get information about my family tree?

Slovene Genealogic Society, Lipce 7, 4220 Škofja Loka should be the right address. This is a voluntary association of genealogists in the field of family and other genealogies.
Their website address is: http://www2.arnes.si/~rzjtopl/rod/rod.htm

## Where do I get birth, marriage and death certificates and divorce results?

Any large municipality in Slovenia has its own government office called Administrative Authority of the Republic of Slovenia, which is responsible for issuing personal documents, IDs, passports, driving licenses etc. within its administrative area.

# History

# Some important milestones in the Slovene history

- the ancestors of Slovenes first settled down in this area
in the **6th century**;

- **7th century**: Carantanian duchy, the first Slovene state;

- **745**: Carantania becomes a part of the Frankish state. Slavs are converted to Christianity and are slowly losing their independence;

- **10th century**: Freising manuscripts, the oldest written record in the Slovene language;

- **14th century up to 1918**: Slovene provinces come under Habsburg dominion and later Austro-Hungarian Monarchy; mid 15th century – a short period of the Counts of Cilli; this was the last principality with its centre in the Slovene territory;

- the Reformation Period lays down foundations for the beginning of the Slovene literary tradition; Slovenes get their first printed book in the Slovene language in **1550** and the first Slovene translation of the Bible in **1584**;

- **1809-13**: the period of Illyrian Provinces (half of Slovenia is under the French Empire) – Slovenes are increasingly becoming aware of their national identity;

- **1848**: a national programme arises among Slovenes, demanding a unification of Slovenes in a single kingdom within the Austrian Monarchy;

- **1918**: World War I is over. When aspirations to divide the Habsburg monarchy into three parts ( Austrian, Hungarian and South Slavic respectively) fail, the Austro-Hungarian Monarchy crumbles. Slovene ethnic territory is apportioned among four states; in the Kingdom of Serbs, Croats and Slovenes (Kingdom of Yugoslavia) Slovene territory is first divided into two administrative units (those of Ljubljana and Maribor) to be later unified in the Drava Banate;

- **1919**: annexation of Prekmurje to the Kingdom of Serbs, Croats and Slovenes;

- **29th November 1945**: Slovenes get their own republic within the Federal People's Republic of Yugoslavia;

- **15th September 1947**: Paris Peace Treaty brings a renewed unification of a great part of the Primorsko region to Slovenia;

- **April 1990**: first democratic elections are held;

- **December 1990**: a referendum for a sovereign and independent state of Slovenia is held (88,5% of votes were cast "for");

- **25th June 1991**: Slovenia proclaims its independence;

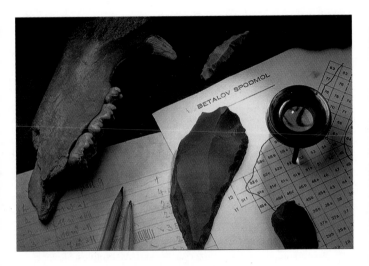

# Where are archeological sites?

Prehistoric sites are scattered around Slovenia and cover a vast area stretching from the mountain Štalenska gora in Koroško to Kapitelj fields near Novo Mesto, Korovci in Goričko and sites along the Adriatic coast. Among them the cave Potočka zijalka under the mountain Olševa has a special place. Excavations and findings by Srečko Brodar, PhD, have won world fame.

Or the findings in the cave Divja Baba near Idrija. A bone flute excavated here is supposedly the oldest musical instrument in the world!

In Vače near Litija there is an Iron Age archeological site. In 1822, a peasant Grilc came across a *situla* – a home-made bronze bucket-like vessel from the end of the 6th century. The *situla* got its name after the place where it was found thus the Vače *situla*.
Geographically, Vače is the centre of Slovenia. It is increasingly depicted in state and national symbols and becoming more and more attractive for tourists.

The *situla*, the bone flute and the majority of the finds are kept in the Slovenian Museum of Natural History in Ljubljana. Special exhibitions present the period of time when mammoth walked the Earth or prehistoric pile dwellers inhabited the Ljubljana Marshes.
http://www2.pms-lj.si/

## What is Claustra Alpinum Iuliarium?

For 500 years the territory of what is today Slovenia was under immediate Roman rule. Even then it was of immense strategic importance as the easiest passage from the Pannonian Plain or Central Europe to the Mediterranean basin, and therefore to the heart of Roman.

To protect themeselves the Romans erected a 150 km long fortified line of defence in this area called Claustra Alpinum Iuliarium.

## Where was the famous battle between two Roman emperors held, which divided the Roman Empire in 394?

In 394, a famous battle of two Roman emperors, Theodosius and Eugenius, was held in the valley Vipavska dolina near the place Ad Frigidum lying between Vipava and Ajdovščina. Both armies counted 50,000 men. The great Roman Empire was divided in two halves then: the Western, which soon collapsed in 476 and Eastern – Byzantine Empire, which remained for almost a thousand years.

# How did Carantania come to existance?

The period between the 5th and 10th century is known as the time of great migrations of peoples in Europe. This time span includes the arrival of Slavs to the Eastern Alps i.e. the territory, where Slovenes live today. According to historical records, the colonisation of Slovenes proceeded from two directions: N to S through the Morava Gate in the Czeck Republic and S to N. The tribes moved from the Pannonian Plain along the valleys of large rivers and reached the sources of the Sava, Drava, Mura and Adige.

By 580, the territory of the upper Sava and Savinja rivers was settled and by 590, that of the upper Drava and Zilja.

In the time of Prince Samo and his tribal union the oldest Slavic statelike formation came to existence. It's name was Carantania and it was an independent duchy till 745. It's center was in the Krn castle just above Celovec (Klagenfurt) gently rising to the west of the plain Gosposvetsko polje (Saalfeld).

# What does the Constitution of the USA have in common with Slovenia?

Until 1414, a special ceremony of enthroning princes of Carantania was preserved in the Slovene language. Later, they were replaced by Carinthian dukes. Original democracy, a political system that is an ideal of any progressive society, and a unique ceremony!

This is the historical heritage of Carinthia, which is often referred to as the "cradle of Slovenehood ". This first-rate and unique type of democracy served as a model for the father of the first American Constitution – Jefferson.

# What is the difference between the stone of the prince and the throne of the duke?

**The stone of the prince** is the remaining part of a Roman pillar. It is displayed in a museum in Klagenfurt, Austria.

**The throne of the duke** is made of rather simply arranged blocks of rock. It served as a symbol of the duke's power and the independence of Carantania.

# How were the dukes of Carantania enthroned?

When the time came for a new duke to ascend the throne, a peasant came who inherited the right to sit on the stone of the prince. This was a round stone that stood in the open near the Krn castle. Round it people gathered. Then the future duke approached, dressed like a peasant, in the company of knights and noblemen. On one side of the duke a black ox was driven and on his other side a skinny horse.

When the peasant sitting on the stone saw the duke, he shouted: Who is the man who is approaching me in such an arrogant manner?"

The people retorted: "The duke of our country is coming."

The peasant asked: "Is he a fair judge and continuous maker of our country's prosperity?"

The people retorted: "He is and will be."

After that the duke had to promise the peasant to be righteous. Upon that the peasant asked him:

"What right do you have to claim this throne?"

"You will be paid 60 farthings, this ox and horse are yours to keep and so is this duke's attire and your family shall pay no duty."

Then the peasant slapped the duke on his cheek and reminded him of his promise to be a fair judge. He descended from the stone and took the animals.

Thereupon the duke sat on the stone, swang his sword in all four directions and promised his people to be a good and fair judge.

After that there was a ceremony in St. Peter's Church. The duke was allowed to remove his farmer's clothes.

The noblemen and knights dined with the duke. Then they set off to the duke's throne in the plain Gosposvetsko polje. The duke mounted it facing east and bareheaded. With his fingers raised he swore to the nobility and promised them all their old rights and graces. Finally, the noble men paid him compliments and presented gifts to him while the duke symbolically distributed his feudal estates among them.

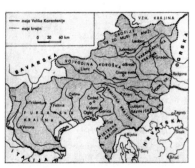

When this was over, they all proceeded to the Church of Gospa Sveta (Maria Saal). The ceremony was completed.

## When and how did Slovenes turn to Christianity?

Around 745, Carantanians came under the Frankish state and in closer contact with Christianity .

The new religion was willingly accepted by the nobility as it strengthened their power and authority. Common people were mostly against it and soon there were two uprisings, both of which were suppressed by the prince Hotimir.

After his death in 769 a fierce revolt broke out which was crushed by the Bavarian duke Tasilo in 772. After the uprising in 820 Carantania lost its status of a duchy and became a county of the Frankish state.

An increasing number of missionaries from Salzburg emerged. They used shrewd methods in converting old pagan religious ways into more Christian ones. The language of the people was preserved and domestic social rivalries were used to serve their purpose. Since they could not do away with old pagan rituals (*koledovanje*, *jurjevanje*, *kresovanje*, Christmas and others) they adapted them to fit the new religion and replaced pagan gods with their saints.

## When did Slovenes get their first writen record?

Freising manuscripts are three Slovene religious forms written at the end of the 10th century.

Three Slovene religious liturgies, which are written in the Latin script, belonged to a Freising bishop Abraham (died in 994). The texts show a demanding ecclesiactical-literary form. They are kept in the Bavarian State Archives in Munich, Germany.

# What are *tabori*?

In his Glory of the Duchy of Carniola, the baron Janez Vajkard Valvasor (1641-1693) wrote the following lines:

"Rocks or natural caves that would serve as shelters are not to be found everywhere; therefore, following examples from nature and their neighbouring countries the dilligent people of Carniola put up fortresses in suitable places to protect themselves from thieving, plundering and other types of hostile activities. Such buildings, which were special kinds of shelters, were called *tabori*. The Czeck, Polish and other nations of Salvic origin called such fortified structures camps, which were erected in chosen places to defend themselves if the enemy was closing in.

A somewhat fortified structure can serve a dual purpose: firstly, that of a fortress and secondly, that of a shelter for refugees, where they can protect themselves and their belongings. Therefore, a *tabor* in Carniola means a fortified structure which is used for storing furniture and sheltering people in times of danger.

In Carniola many such fortresses were built, which is clear evidence that the people of this country suffered many wars and raids and saw moving of troops."

Many fortresses were built by erecting a fortified wall round an existing church on top of a hill if that hill was suitable for defence.

A *tabor* near Hrastovlje under Črni Kal (picture) is most interesting. The pilgrim's church was built in the 12th century; the walls date back in the 16th century; the church is famous for its fresco, which depicts a variant of the famous Dance of Death motif.

## Why do most Protestants live in Prekmurje?

The wave of peasant uprisings that hit Europe in the 15th and 16th century reached Slovene parts as well. Peasants demanded their "old right" which was laid down in an *urbar,* a book of subjects and their duties to the lord.

The soon following Protestant movement which started in Germany came to Slovene parts as well. This period is of particular importance in Slovene history, as Slovenes got their first two books, *Katekizem* (The Cathecism) and *Abecednik* (The Alphabet Book). In 1555, a law was passed in Augsburg that all subjects should be of the same religion as their sovereign. Consequently, many Protestants

had to sell their property and leave the Habsburg Empire.

Slovene Protestant nobility left too and with them their knowledge and capital. This vacancy was filled by Italian families that had bought their titles, local townspeople and even farmers. In Prekmurje, which was under Hungarian rule at that time, Protestants were not persecuted.

## When did Slovenes get their translation of the Bible?

Slovenes got their first translation of the Bible in 1584 and were the seventh European nation who had the book of books written in their mother tongue.

The Bible was named after its translator, Jurij Dalmatin (1547-1589), a Protestant preacher and writer.

Unfortunately, most copies of Dalmatin's Bible were burnt by Catholic priests in their desire to crush the Protestant movement (1600-1601) and only few copies were preserved.

# Which Slovene was already a member of the British Royal Society?

The baron Janez Vajkard Valvasor (1641-1693), a member of glorious Carniolan nobility and the captain of the Lower Carniolan army published The Glory of the Duchy of Carniola in 1689. His vivid description of the seasonal lake Cerkniško jezero and relating karst phenomena aroused great interest among the then scientists. On account of his work the baron became a member of the British Royal Society.

Pletrje                    Stična

## Is monastic life still popular in Slovenia?

The Church played an important part in the history of Slovene people – monasteries in particular. In the 12th century five monasteries were built in the territory of what is today Slovenia occupied by four monastic orders. A century later the number of monasteries was twenty-one and that of monastic orders doubled. The number continued to grow in the following years. Monasteries were crucial for the development of medieval towns though a great many were closed in the years 1780 -1790.

**The most prominent and active monasteries in Slovenia are:**
Monastery of Carthusian monks Pleterje near Šentjernej,
Monastery of Cistercian monks in Stična near Ivančna Gorica,
Monastery of Minorites in Ptuj.

# Where was the greatest
# mountain battle of all time held?

World War I left deep scars in the hearts of Slovenes. Its death toll was high and many lives were destroyed on the front. At the dawn of the 20th century Austria was the homeland of Slovenes.
The greatest mountain battle ever lasted from May 1915 to November 1917.

The war between Austria-Hungary and Italy was sparked off by Italy's entering into the TRIPLE ALLIANCE (London Treaty).

Soldiers fighting on either side of the Soča front were of more than 20 different nationalities. The front line ran from Rombon and the Krn mountain range to Gorica and from the Kras to the Gulf of Trieste. 300,000 soldiers were killed and many more were injured.

There were 12 offensives altogether. The first eleven, which were led by Italians, could not break through the defence line. In the final one, the Austrians attacked and drove the Italians deep into Italy.

## How many lives did the road construction work over the mountain pass Vršič claim?

The mountain pass Vršič (1611 m) in the Julian Alps was the only posible way to bring supplies to the Austro-Hungarian army in this part of the Soča front.
Russian POWs from Galicia were used to construct the road. Due to the cold winter, adverse weather conditions and avalanches 10,000 Russian prisoners died while building the road across Vršič.

Russian chapel

# What do the cities of Rome, Vienna, Paris, Budapest, Belgrade, Aachen and Berlin have in common with Ljubljana?

Today, Ljubljana is the capital of Slovenia, but it was not always so in the past. In ancient times Rome was its capital. Then it was Aachen for a very long time.

As unbelievable as it may seem, all the above mentioned cities used to be capital cities of Slovenes in different periods of time.

## How old is the Slovene railway?

It was not until the arrival of the steam locomotive in the first half of the 19th century that the problem of cheap transport of larger quantities of goods was solved. That was the first step in assuring a successful and dynamic development of any economy. In England it caused the industrial revolution and soon Europe and America followed.

Austria-Hungary got its first railway in 1837. In 1846, a link was constructed to Celje in the Slovenia of today i.e. only 16 years after the revolutionary success of George and Robert Stephenson in England. Naturally, Slovenia did not get its railway in order to promote the country's local economy. Austria needed it to connect Vienna with the port of Trieste. The railway reached Ljubljana in 1849 and Trieste in 1857.

# Why was Hospital Franja such a phenomenon?

During World War II Slovenia was occupied by three enemy armies: the Germans occupied Gorenjsko and Štajersko, the Hungarians Prekmurje and the Italians occupied whatever territory was left.

On 27th April 1941, soon after occupation, the enemy was met by an organized all-Slovene resitance. At the beginning of the freedom fight nobody had the necessary knowledge and experience with the injured, i.e. where to treat them and how. Till then army doctors were used to working under different conditions: fronts were determined, hinterland was safe, means of transport were plenty. Nothing was the same here. There were neither drugs, sanitary materials nor trained staff.

The problem was ingeniously solved by building hidden partisan hospitals. Some were only makeshift shelters or wooden barracs. Nonetheless, the main purpose was achieved: the troops were relieved of the burden of their injured fellow-soldiers and the former had much better conditions to recover safely hidden from the enemy.

The Hospital Franja or Slovene Partisan Army Hospital Franja is remarkable in many ways. 522 injured soldiers were treated there from the autumn 1943 till the final liberation. This was in the heart of occupied Europe, in the fascist Reich!

The Hospital Franja, which has preserved its original image, is hidden in the narrow Pasice ravine near Cerkno. It is still open - not to wounded partisans though - but to masses of visitors from all over the world who do not try to conceal their respect or admiration when they see it.

## Why is Begunje in the Gorenjsko region called: "Town of a sad memory "?

Begunje is a small town at the foot of the Karavanke mountain range. The village originates from the 11th century.

In the middle of a large fenced park in the village there raises a mansion Katzenstein. Many nobles owned it in the past. Later the premises was turned into a women's prison managed by the Sisters nuns of the Society of St. Vincent of Paul.

During World War II the mansion was used as a gestapo prison. From 1941-1945 more than 12,000 Slovenes were imprisoned there. The Gestapo sent innocent people and children to Begunje. And despite the fact that they were not involved in the resistance movement they were massively killed in the near valley Draga – ten of them for every fallen German soldier in Gorenjsko.The Gestapo had the same programme in a prison in Celje called *Celjski pisker* or a Celje pot.

Today, a part of the prison in the extension of the mansion is turned into a memorial museum. In the near-by valley Draga the graves of the killed Slovene hostages are well tended.

# The Slovene language, literature and school system

# Where are Slovene courses?

**The Centre for Slovene as a Second/Foreign Language** extends the understanding of the Slovene language, literature and culture on an international scale. It also encourages international research in Slovene language and literature, organises professional and scientific conferences and develops the complete infrastructure for attaining, examining and certifying proficiency in Slovene as a second/foreign language.

The programme offers a varied selection of language courses, differing in length (from 20 to 560 hours), intensity and goals. The most popular courses are those that combine language learning with studying modern culture and society in Slovenia. These are the Summer, One-Year and Winter Schools of Slovene Language which are of particular interest to participants from abroad.

The University of Ljubljana, The Faculty of Arts
The Centre for Slovene as a Second/Foreign Language
Aškerčeva 2, SI-1001 Ljubljana
http://www.ff.uni-lj.si/center-slo/

# How is Slovene written and pronounced?

Slovene differs greatly from other Slavic languages. Even Croats and Serbs do not understand it though the languages are quite similar. Slovene vocabulary includes some very old words. The writing is not phonetic and a spoken word is often quite different from the written one. The Slovene language has preserved dual number, a rarity among the Indoeuropean languages. It includes many reduced vowels and tongue twisters:

**prst** (finger) , **trst** (reed), **pešci** (pedestrians), **čez cestišče** (across the road)...

The Slovene alphabet has 25 letters. It does not have the letters W, Q, X, Y. But it has three new letters: Č (pronounced as *ch* in English, e.g. chocolate), Š (*sh, as in sh*ock), and Ž (*zh*, as in azure). The mark ˇ above the letters is called a carrot, or, in Slovenian, *strešica* (literally: little roof). The letter C is pronounced as ts, e.g. tzar. The Slovene R is pronounced strongly, slightly rolled. It is pronounced as er when it stands before another consonant or when it stands between two consonants as in *prst*. L and V at the end of a word or before another consonant are pronounced like English *w (vol̯k (wol̯f)* – *kno̯w)*. D and Ž together are pronounced like English *j (Madžarska (Hungary)* – *Jane)*:

# Who is the most prominent Slovene poet and writer?

**France Prešeren** (1800-1849)
Prešeren's poetry was born in a time when Slovene literature was practicaly non-existent. Modest literary efforts by Vodnik were merely a beginning, hence Prešeren had no real predecessor. His poetry coined in Slovene was of great value and importance for this country, where German was then the official language. You will rarely find masterpieces like *A Toast, The Baptism at The Savica, Sonnets of Unhappiness* etc. in world literature.

However, Prešeren's work and importance was not recognized during his lifetime. Only 20 years after his death was the poet duly appreciated. Since then, his work has always been in the centre of everything beautiful and noble that this nation has created.

**Ivan Cankar** (1879-1918)
Though phisically feeble, Ivan Cankar was a strong person in spirit. He was intelligent and competent, paradoxical, ironic and sarcastic. He was inclined to daydreaming and flights of imagination. Moreover, he was very emotional and sentimental. This prolific writer, who kept retiring into his world of imagination, grew into an outstanding social critic. He was the first Slovene writer who earned his daily bread exclusively by writing.

Each of his works is a pearl in Slovene literature and drama and Cankar himself a master writer:
Literature: Bailiff Yerney and His Right, The Ward of Our Lady of Mercy, White Chrysanthemum, On the Hill, Dream Visions ...
Dramas: Farm-Hands, King on Betajnova, For Nation's Welfare, Scandal in the Šentflorjan Valley ...

# What is the Slovene school system like?
## Primary school education

is provided at elementary schools, elementary schools with adapted programme and educational institutions for children with special needs. For non-Slovene residents there is an international school in English.

### Secondary school education
is divided into general, vocational and professional education. Grammar school education ends with a matura exam, which is a form of external examination.
Short-term vocational education and secondary vocational education is completed with a school-leaving examination; secondary technical education ends with a vocational matura.

## How many universities are there in Slovenia?

The beginnings of schooling in the Slovene language coincided with the Reformation movement, when Slovenes got their first Slovene book. Consequently, the first Slovene grammar schools were opened: in Klagenfurt (1553) and Ljubljana (1563).
With the arrival of the Jesuites in the first half of the 17th century higher education was possible in Ljubljana.
Today, there are two universities and several colleges in Slovenia. 88,000 students are entered.

### The University of Ljubljana
Kongresni trg 12, SI-1000 Ljubljana
http://www.uni-lj.si

### The University of Maribor
Slomškov trg 15, SI-2000 Maribor
http://www.uni-lj.si

By completing undergraduate studies (4 to 6 years) students obtain either university or college education (3 to 4 years). Post-graduate studies, which are a follow-up of univeristy studies, are of a different duration: 1 to 2 years (graduate professional training), 2 years (master's degree) and 4 years (PhD degree).

# What is SAZU?

The Slovene Academy of Sciences and Arts - SAZU was established some three hundred years ago and is by far the oldest academy of its kind.

The Academia operosorum was founded in 1693. In the first eight years 23 scientists claimed its membership. The Academia's first president was a PhD in cannon law, provost, protonotary apostolic, count palatine, scientist and poet Janez Krstnik Prešeren (1656-1704).

The members of the Academia operosorum made their first public appearance in 1701. The solemn event took place in a richly adorned hall of the bishop's palace.

In the first years of the Academia a number of books and discussions about history, homeland, biographies, jurisprudence, medicine, nature and astrology were preserved. These works made up a scientific and literary presentation of Slovenes in a Europe where national identity was not yet awakened. The Slovene Academy of Sciences and Arts is therefore a part of the legacy of the Slovene people.

# Are there different dialects?

Slovene has many different dialects, which may differ from town to town. Nonetheless, there are eight main Slovene dialects spoken in Slovenia and its neighbouring countries:

1. the Pannonian dialect
2. the Štajersko dialect
3. the Koroško dialect
4. the Gorenjsko dialect
5. the Dolenjsko dialect
6. the Kočevsko dialect
7. the Rovtarsko dialect
8. the Primorsko dialect

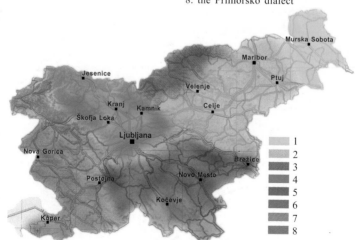

# Politics and Legislation

# What is Slovenia's political order?

Official name:The Republic of Slovenia
It is a democratic republic based on the principle of separation of powers
between legislature, executive and judiciary.

### The President of the Republic
Represents the Republic of Slovenia and is the Commander in Chief of its
armed forces. The president is elected for a five-year term by direct
elections. The president can hold his office only twice.

### The National Assembly
Is the state legislative body comprising 90 deputies that passes laws.

### The National Council
(40 members) is a body of persons designated to act in an advisory
capacity and representing social, economic, trade and professional and
local interests.

### The Goverment
comprising the Prime Minister and the ministers of state, is the bearer of
executive power and accountable to the National Assembly.

### The Courts
Judges independently exercise their duties but in accordance with the
consitution and the law. There are four levels of courts of general
jurisdiction: country and district courts; higher courts are courts of
appeallate jurisdiction and the supreme court is the highest court in the
judicial system.

### The Constitution of the Republic of Slovenia
On December 23 rd, 1991, the Assembly of the Republic of Slovenia
adopted the Constitution of the Republic of Slovenia based on a
parliamentary form of national authority. Je najvišji pravni akt, ki ga
sprejema in dopolnjuje državni zbor po posebnem postopku (potrebna je
dvotretjinska večina).

### Laws
Other legal acts following in a hierarchical order are: laws passed by the
National Assembly, Government ordinances for implementing laws,
regulations, guidelines and decrees by Ministries for implementing laws
and observing Government ordinances and regulations by local self-
administration bodies, which are passed in order to settle local matters.

# What is the history of Slovene political parties?

Historically, the formation of political parties in Slovenia falls into two basic periods. The first began at the end of the 19th century with the formation of the main parties of a political spectrum such as which arose in the other lands of Central Europe. This period ended with World War II.

The second period began at the end of the 1980s. Formally, the process of formation of political parties was given way to with adoption of amendments to the Constitution in September 1989. The classification of parties can be as follows:
- parties formed by intelectuals joined in protest to the then Yugoslavia,
- parties formed of professional organizations or trade groups,
- parties formed of "former" social-political organizations in power.

The latter stressed breaking with their tradition and searched for a new identity.

## Prominent Slovene political parties:

Liberal Democratic Party
Trg Republike 3
SI-1001 Ljubljana
http://www.lds.si/

Slovene National Party
Kotnikova 2
SI-1000 Ljubljana
http://www.sns.si/

Slovene People's Party
Beethovnova ulica 4
SI-1000 Ljubljana
http://www.sls.si/

Associated List of Social Democrates
Levstokova 15
SI-1000 Ljubljana
http://www.zlsd.si

New Slovenia
Cankarjeva cesta 11
1000 Ljubljana
http://www.nsi.si/

Greens of Slovenia
Komenskega 11
SI-1000 Ljubljana
http://www.zeleni.si/

## How is the police authority organized?

It's a body within the Ministry of Interior of the Republic of Slovenia. Organisationally, it performs the tasks on a state, regional and local level.

- On a state level: General Police Directorate consisting of 10 internal organisational units.
- On a regional level: 11 Police Directorates located in Celje, Koper, Kranj, Krško, Ljubljana, Maribor, Murska Sobota, Nova Gorica, Novo Mesto, Postojna and Slovenj Gradec.
- On a local level: 99 police stations.

Police forces fall into three units: uniformed and criminal police forces and a special force. There is also a Police Academy working under the auspices of the Police.

General Police Directorate
Štefanova 2, SI-1501 Ljubljana
http://www.policija.si

## What are the traffic regulations in Slovenia?

**Speed limits**
50 kmph in residential areas
90 kmph on all roads if not indicated otherwise
100 kmph on the roads reserved for motor traffic
130 kmph on motorways

**Lights** have to be **turned on** 24 hrs a day.
Fog lights can be turned on only in cases when visibility is less than 50 m.
**Seat belts** are obligatory for a driver and co-driver. Children's seats are obligatory for babies and smaller children.

**Permitted alcohol content in blood** is 0.50 g alcohol per a kilogram of blood.

**The use of mobile phones** is strictly forbidden when driving. Only the use of hands-free mobile phones is permitted.

# Practical advice and useful addresse

## Where do I get VAT refunded?

The value of the purchased goods on one or several receipts issued by the same retailer has to exceed SIT 15,000. The foreign traveller has to obtain a correctly filled in DDV-VP form from the retailer.

VAT can be refunded at 27 border crossings at the offices of KOMPAS MTS, d.d., operating within the system GLOBAL REFUND.

## Where can I obtain post office price lists, information on philatelic clubs and Slovene stamps?

The Post of Slovenia has a branched network of post offices in all Slovene towns that provide postal, telephonic and telegraphic services. You can also find an agency of the Postal Bank of Slovenia in all post offices.  http://www.posta.si/

Slovenian Philatelic Association
p.p. 1584
si-1001 Ljubljana
http://www.zveza-fzs.si/

**Did you know that ...**
... more than 100 years ago a Slovene, Lovrenc Košir, suggested a simpler way of paying postal services, but was ignored?
An Englishman, Rowland Hill, is officially recognized as the creator of a stamp, while Košir spent his whole life trying in vain to prove that he was the inventor.

# Where do I get the address of...

### The President of Slovenia
Office of the President of the Republic of Slovenia
Erjavčeva 1, SI-1000 Ljubljana
http://www.sigov.si/up-rs/

### Slovene Parliament
Šubičeva 4, SI-1000 Ljubljana
http://www.dz-rs.si/si/home.html

### Ambassies
### Ministry of Foreign Affairs
Prešernova cesta 25
SI-1000 Ljubljana
http://www.sigov.si/mzz/

### Wellfare organisations
RED CROSS
Mirje 19
SI - 1000 Ljubljana
**Napaka! Zaznamek ni določen.**

SLOVENE CARITAS
Kristanova ulica 1
SI-1000 Ljubljana
http://www.karitas.si/

### TV stations
Svet za radiodifuzij, Kotnikova 19a, SI-1000 Ljubljana
http://www.sigov.si/srd/main341.html

Museums
ARNES – Academic and research net of Slovenia
http://www2.arnes.si/~ljprirodm6/

# Questions about Slovenia

## Facts and Figures

## Customs and Tradition

## Free time, food and drinks

## Geographical characteristics

## Tourist information and locations

# History

# The Slovene language, literature and school system

# Politics and Legislation

# Practical advice and useful addresse

**The booklet has been translated into Slovenian, English, German and Italian.**

## Questions about Slovenia

It provides answers to numerous questions about Slovenia and Slovenes living in their native and neighbouring countries as well as abroad.

The booklet is about holidays, wine, the sea, mountains, forests, rivers, early and recent history, cuisine, tourism, the legal system, politics, humour, envy, cleverness, sadness, drinking problems, superstition...

*(112 pages, 150 colour photographs, a map, format 11.5 x 22.5 cm, paperback)*

## Slovenian Cooking

The booklet details 140 old and not so old national dishes, which cherish a rich tradition in Slovenia. Throughout the centuries some of them have managed to preserve themselves to this day. A different ground structure and varying climate in some areas as well as economic and cultural factors have contributed their part in creating 40 culinary regions. These are characterized by different eating habits and typical dishes.

140 recipes of both very well and less known Slovene dishes have been collected by a chef, Andrej A. Fritz, 2001

*(64 pages, format 11.5 x 22.5 cm, paperback)*

## Slovenia - Guide

The booklet is a brief presentation of Slovenia and its principal characteristics. The texts are complemented by 150 colour photographs and a small but clear map of Slovenia.

The introductory part is general, and includes basic information about Slovenia, its tourism, history, arts and crafts, cuisine... The following chapters present individual regions, bigger towns and other sights of interest.

*(112 pages, 150 colour photographs, a map, format 11.5 x 22.5 cm, paperback)*

## A road map of Slovenia and Istria

Maps of the following city centres: Ljubljana, Maribor, Celje, Kranj and Koper
*(scale:1:300,000, format 100 x 70)*

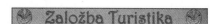

Trstenik 101 SI-4204 Golnik
e-mail: info@zalozba-turistika.si
www.zalozba-turistika.si

CAVE–GROTTA-HÖHLE

# SVETA JAMA

(Koper, grad-castle Socerb)

**SVETNIKOVO ZAVETIŠČE**
**IL RIFUGIO DEL SANTO**
**SAINTS REFUGE**
**HEILIGES HORT**

JAMA-GROTTA-CAVE-HÖHLE

# D I M N I C E

(HRPELJE-KOZINA, SLIVJE)

VRAŽJA PREKAJEVALNICA MESA
**L'AFFUMICATOIO DEL DIAVOLO**
DEVILS SMOKEHOUSE
**TEUFELS RAUCHKAMMER**

**Informacije-informations:**
http://www2.arnes.si/~kpjdd2/

phone, fax.:00386 (0)5 6526036;
gsm: 00386 41 693014
**e-mail:** franc.maleckar@guest.arnes.si

**UPRAVITELJ – MANAGER**:
SPELEO CLUB DIMNICE,
P.P. 74, 6001 KOPER